T0065332

# Love Addiction

## Love Poems

Traci J. Hinds

authorHOUSE®

*AuthorHouse™*
*1663 Liberty Drive*
*Bloomington, IN 47403*
*www.authorhouse.com*
*Phone: 1 (800) 839-8640*

*© 2016 Traci Hinds. All rights reserved.*

*No part of this book may be reproduced, stored in a retrieval system, or transmitted by any means without the written permission of the author.*

*Published by AuthorHouse  01/30/2016*

*ISBN: 978-1-5049-6278-0 (sc)*
*ISBN: 978-1-5049-6279-7 (e)*

*Print information available on the last page.*

*Any people depicted in stock imagery provided by Thinkstock are models, and such images are being used for illustrative purposes only. Certain stock imagery © Thinkstock.*

*This book is printed on acid-free paper.*

*Because of the dynamic nature of the Internet, any web addresses or links contained in this book may have changed since publication and may no longer be valid. The views expressed in this work are solely those of the author and do not necessarily reflect the views of the publisher, and the publisher hereby disclaims any responsibility for them.*

*Scripture quotations marked NKJV are taken from the New King James Version. Copyright © 1982 by Thomas Nelson, Inc. Used by permission. All rights reserved.*

# Contents

# Acknowledgements

Special thanks to Lascelle for his encouragement and support. Thanks to my editing team Angela, Janice, and Laurie. Thank you Leslie for always screaming, "if not now when !". Thank you Luis for helping me overcome my fear. Thank you Dad and my sons Jelani and Omari for supporting me and loving me unconditionally.

# Introduction

I have been writing about love since I was nine years old. Of course the work at the precious age of nine is not worthy of being in this book, however that work is what led to the birth of this book.

For as long as I could remember I was in love with love. I have always dreamed of having my own love story to tell. As a little girl I loved seeing and hearing love stories. My love stories were mostly made up in my vivid imagination and in my dreams.

My parents were separated and divorced by the time I was five years old. I vaguely remember living with both my parents. Needless to say there was no love story in my household to be told.

I watched my mother go through different phases of love but never the story I wanted. Ultimately as a child you want your parents to be the example of the love story you want to tell. You want your parents to stay married forever and love each other forever. That was not my story. My friend's parents, The Nanton's, Pigford's, Redd's and countless others unknowingly became that love story for me. All of my friend's parents were living the ultimate love story as far as my immature young mind could see.

Love comes in many seasons and it is different for each individual. This book is a reflection of the deep emotions I have had along the way as I loved from a young lady into the woman I am today. I've had four great loves in my life but no doubt there was one undeniable love of my life.

The poems in this book reflect the mixed emotions I experienced while loving the loves of my life. There are several poems that helped me verbalize pain and helped me release that pain to love again. My hope is that the reader can relate to the pain and also feel relief from the pain and see happiness when it presents itself. I want the reader to know that love is always just around the corner you just have to believe.

# Dedication

To my motivator, my rock, my voice of reason, my teacher, my everything, my mother Bonnie Taylor (October 1, 1938 – August 26, 1986)

Typically each year in the weeks leading up to October 1st, I am a mess, overwhelmed with sadness, emptiness, and loneliness. Although many years have passed the pain is sometimes so fresh and present. Writing has helped release some of that pain.

Every year in October I pray I make it through without shedding a tear and becoming undone. In the last hour the flood gates are opened and I slip into that place. That place of wishing she was here, wishing I had my mother's shoulder to lean on, wishing I could share my love stories with her, wishing she knew all my friends, wishing she knew him as the man he is today, wishing I could tell her my cares and worries as I did when I was a girl and a young adult. My mother had all the answers for me. She had a way of making sense out of every situation regardless of the unsettling facts that may surround the situation.

As I try to make sense of the sadness I feel I know my sadness is not selfish or simply that I miss her so much. My sadness is entwined in knowing what my children and my granddaughter have missed. Sadden because all the riches my mother passed to me; my children, her grandchildren, and her great-grandchild will not be showered with the fullness of their grandmother and all her greatness. She was a strong, positive, kind, and loving woman. I celebrate the memory of her life through my writing.

Love experiences told through poetry
from one woman's perspective

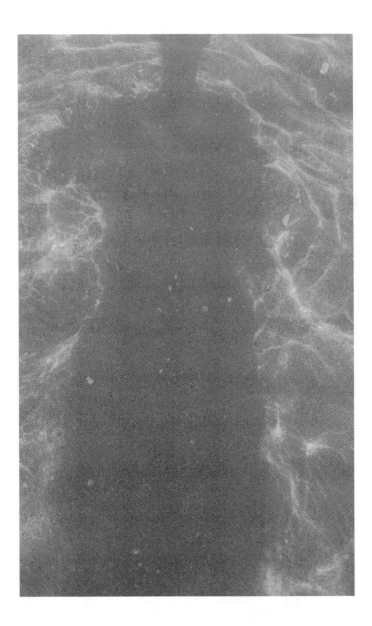

# Reflections 1987

I see a woman

A woman full of love ready to explode.
Sometimes I wonder will this woman ever unload.
A lover here, a lover there when will I find a love that is crystal clear.

I see a woman

A woman ready to share
but to share is sometimes so hard to bear.
To open your heart and let someone in…

I see a woman from within.

# Barricaded Heart ( I )

Who would have thought one could feel like a teen,
the idea of dating was not so keen.

In the strong hold of my mind I spent a decade,
building around my heart a barricade.
A structure so strong and so tall, in an instant I lost it all.

Who would have thought you'd catch me off guard,
fighting now will be too hard.

I can feel again in that special place,
what move did you make to get in my space!

Who would have thought?

# I LOVE YOU

He said I LOVE YOU
does he know what that means
should I say I love him too so it seemed.

He said I LOVE YOU
does he know loving me is an emotional scene
unconditional love is what I mean.

Will he love me with finesse
or will he be like all the rest?

I LOVE YOU,
eight little letters so simple but yet so complicated.

My desire is for him to stay
I wonder if he'll run astray.

Eight little letters He said.

I LOVE YOU!

# I Want You

I want to feel you touch me.
I want to feel your hand in my hand.
I want to feel your lips on my lips.
I want to feel the heat of your body warm my body.
I want your hands to message every inch of my body.
I want your soft wet lips to kiss every surface of my body.
I want to touch you, your face, and your body from head to toe.

I lay at night and dream of the day that I will feel you inside me.
I wait patiently with anticipation.
As I sleep I can see our bodies move as one.
I imagine making love to you every day.

I WANT YOU!!!

# Weak Heart

My heart is heavy laden and my heart is weak
I spend too much time unable to fall asleep.
I dream of a day when my heart can rest.
In that space where there will be no more tests.

My mind is heavy laden and my heart is weak
I've got to take this life of mine and make my stake.
There is a life that I know exists somehow there is always a twist.
Bending here and bending there somehow
I'm consumed with bending everywhere.

My mind is heavy laden and my heart is weak
I spend time on my knees asking what was my mistake.
The answer is crystal clear I hear a voice that says
I think you know my dear.
Stay on your knees and I'll be pleased.

My mind is heavy laden and my heart is weak.

# Barricaded Heart ( II )

Who would have thought it would end like this
for a few weeks I enjoyed companion bliss.

I should have known what felt so right
would end in merely one night,
here I am with such a long fight,
an internal struggle that will require astounding might.

Who would have thought you'd catch me off guard
Fighting now will be so hard.

Forced to build another structure, so strong and so tall
praying I don't lose it all.

Here I am again in the strong hold of my mind
building around my heart a barricade,
wasting what will seem like a decade.

Who would have thought?

# Old and Gray

I enjoy being in your space
I can't wait to see your face.

I can still smell you, not the showered fresh you
but the you that was inside me.

Baby I got plans for us
I hope you will stay on the bus
and ride this one out
life will be grand without a doubt.

I want to wipe your ass when you are old and gray
and depend on you to treat me the same way.

# Blue Sand

Here I sit on the sand,
and right before me the sun stands.

The wind is in my hair blowing in the breeze,
the sun warms my body with ease.

The roar of the ocean behind my ears,
this is what I waited for, for many years.

To share this time with you,
makes me forget when I was blue.

# Splash

I had an intimate encounter today
with an old delightful force of nature,
we knew each other well.
I wondered why I've stayed away so long.
As I sit on God's playground
the blanket of the sun warms my cold defense.
I find myself wide open,
meditating on the sound of the sea
crashing into the playground.
It is in this place where I feel the most at home
safe and protected by nature.
I am presented with crystal clear aqua blue treasures.
I can hear the waves calling my name *T R A C I,*

Come, get quenched and soothe your body's thirst.
The sea is calm ready to receive me
SPLASH!

# What Will I Write

I sit in front of my keyboard and my head is full of words and thoughts. I am compelled to write. Wondering what will prevail. In an instant I become overwhelmed with choosing what exactly will I write.

I have the whispers of politics in my head and the injustices of others on everyday common things that should be a simple right. I think often about LOVE. I wonder if I am obsessed with LOVE. I think of my children and how my love for them is so full. Then I drift on to work and career. I think about the love I have for children and the innate need and want I have to teach, but struggle with fully motivating myself to move in that direction once and for all.

Then in the darkest space I think of the thing that saddens me no matter when or where. I think of DEATH. I think of MY MOTHER, my best friend who left me to soon. If I could do one thing it would be to bring her back so I could enjoy her presence again. I long for the ability to know and love my mother as the adult that I am. She left too soon.

I guess today the thing that prevailed was the dark side the side that saddens most.

# <u>SPIRITUAL JOURNEY</u>

The phrase, "Spiritual Journey" has been in my thoughts for some time. What is a Spiritual Journey? How does one have a Spiritual Journey?

Recently I journeyed from one side of the world to another. I took a trip to Korea to visit my love. The trip did not turn out as I thought it would. I am sure it worked out just as God planned. In the bible the word journey is referenced many times. I'm not sure which biblical reference my journey is in line with. I am sure God was the leader in my journey.

While in Korea I traveled from a small town Pyeongtaek to the big city, Seoul by myself. My first move was to pray and ask the Lord to protect me and provide traveling mercies. My prayers gave me peace. I dove into the Korean culture. I took the subway spoke to many strangers using gestures and showing the people the notes I had which referenced the places I wanted to reach. I walked the streets of Seoul taking it all in. I relied on God and the kindness of strangers, strangers that did not speak my language and neither me theirs. In God's infinite wisdom we were able to communicate.

I was on the subway heading back to Pyeongtaek, when the young lady who had given me instruction at the beginning of my two-hour train ride noticed I was not getting off to transfer. I felt her eyes glaring at me. I looked up and her facial expression was that of urgency. She uttered one word, Pyeongtaek! She gestured for me to get up, pointed to the door, and we exited the train together. She pointed to the track where I was to stand. I bowed as a gesture of thanks. She smiled, reached for my hand, we shook hands and she waved good-bye.

I always believed people of all races and cultures were more alike than different regardless of their language or religious beliefs. I also believe people are kind. This trip solidified those beliefs.

Revealed with such clarity, life is what you make it. I saw all walks of life throughout this journey. I talked in-depth to many strangers along the way. What was evident, those that were happy and satisfied with their lives, they chose to be happy regardless of their circumstance or situation. It is easy to sit back and feel sorry for yourself and complain about your life. The hard part is choosing to do something different to make your life more desirable and pleasing unto oneself.

Your state of mind is everything as is your will to improve your circumstances and situation. God has given us His word for peace and hope. (For I know the thoughts that I think toward you, saith the LORD, thoughts of peace and not of evil, to give you an expected end) **Jeremiah 29:11**

There was a time when I thought you could have a journey without physically traveling. My thoughts have been transformed. Today I feel differently. A journey is a mental process which moves you from one mind-set to another. I believe, in order to do this you need to literally remove yourself from your familiar surrounding and submerge in the unknown. Trusting in God as you go through. (**Proverbs 3:5-6**)

I think I just experienced a Spiritual Journey!

# Dragging My Heart Along

I thought I was ready.
I thought I'd be OK.
I thought I would walk out of this
and everything would somehow
mysteriously be OK.

I thought my heart was tired.
I thought my heart had had enough.
I thought my heart was closed to this idea of love.
I thought my heart was ready for another kind of love.
My heart aches for sure.

Now that I am sitting still and thinking,
I realized it's not my heart that is ready
it's my mind, body, and soul that is ready.

I will just have to drag my heart along.
I thank God for my mind, body and soul,
thanks for standing up and protecting my heart.

# Liar Liar

Liar liar pants on fire
that's the school yard sayin
that will always be playin,
cause some brothas are so deep
the only way they balance and see their feet
is to tell you the lies, the sweet sweet lies,
the lies that sound crazy
and make your clear days hazy,
some brothas are so damn lazy.

If only they knew the way to be true
and to secure their shit like crazy glue
is to set themselves free and declare to be,
with just one sista you know Mrs and Mista.
Imagine that, set yourself free and declare to be
with just one sista Mrs and Mista.
Set yourself free and declare to be...

You will then see the bliss you missed
the sweetness of my kiss,
my un-denying love and gratitude
no attitude.
I'll stroke your ego make you feel like a Leo,
Tony the tiger beating your chest declaring,
it's great to be straight.

To be free no more lies, sweet sweet lies,
you've set yourself free to love one sista
now go ahead and ask her
to be your Mrs to compliment Mista.

# Spherical Motions

Life is so busy sometimes it feels like I'm

spinning and spinning and spinning.

It's hard to tell if I'm winning at this game called life.

Everywhere I look there's strife

and life just keeps spinning and spinning and spinning,

around and around in this spherical motion

I have no notion what lurks beyond the deep blue ocean.

Riding the waves of the sphere

boldly with no fear

riding, trusting and thrusting

full speed ahead!

# Naples

As I sit and watch nature unfold
I am forced to put pen to paper
to have a story told.

Nature is the thing I see,
that brings men and women together to just be.

The sun is in the back drop waiting for bed
as the birds fly around waiting to be fed.

The wind is blowing fiercely with great determination.
I hear the languages of the many spectators.
The voices of many nations.

This small moment in time is grand
the world should be here where I stand.

No killing, no fighting, no racists slurs
just one goal, to release a pelican from a life of blur.

This small moment in time is grand
the world should be here where I stand.

# Memory Lane

Taking this walk down memory lane,
all these emotions are so insane.

My mind reveals a place in time
when everything was seemingly fine.

These feelings emerged
as a sweet aged bottle of wine
my heart beats again, oh how devine.

I love a man who was gone for so long
how on earth could that be wrong.

How does my heart work this way,
once I love you I never stray.

It's like my love was on hold,
remembering the mold
that was shaped by your control.

Here we are in this new space and time
thirty three years later
so glad my heart didn't resign.

Taking this walk down memory lane
all these emotions are so insane.

I love a man who was gone for so long
how on earth could that be wrong.

# Twisted Dance

How do I do this, this twisted dance
that one does to protect their heart?
How do I do this, this twisted dance,
that crazy dance so I don't look too eager or too thirsty?
I know the dance and love the music
but somehow this dance escapes me.
Fear keeps me from dancing.
Fear keeps me from dancing the dance
that will expose my very being.
What can I be so fearful of?
Fearful of not feeling the way I do
or having to once again operate on the heart
and do patch work to try and heal.
Terrified that I won't heal this time
and will be forced to not believe in love.
I so believe in love I can't imagine life
without love or the belief in love.
Damnit!
I'm in that place again.
You know that place, that rocky place
where you feel so unsure of love,
not your love but his love
and his ability to love you the way you need to be loved.
How do I do this, this twisted dance
that one does to protect their heart?
How do I do this, this twisted dance,
that crazy dance so I don't look too eager or too thirsty?
How do I do this, how do I do this twisted dance of love.
How do I do this...

# Can He See Me

My mind is constantly drawn to his memory
knowing clearly he's not the enemy.

In my silence he exist unknowingly
present and so ever flowingly.

I can see all of Him.

I can see his heart covered with that tarp
to protect what's been in constant neglect.

I can see all of Him.

His mind is strong and robust
sometimes I think he may actually bust,
bust into tiny little pieces
that I will gladly pick up and put together like a thesis.

Beautiful stature of a man
in all of God's love He stands

I can see all of Him.

Can He see me?

# Coward

If I were not such a coward I'd say I love you.

I love the way you walk, the way you talk
your smile, your quick wit, your brain, sounds so lame.
I love your determination and serenity all with no game.

If I were not such a coward I'd say, I love you.

I wake up thinking of you, day dream about you,
reminisce about all the moments we've spent together
and the adventures we've shared.

If only I dared I'd say I go to sleep thinking of you.
You exist in my dreams such a familiar theme.

Then a thought enters my mind to define.

A true coward is one who awakens another's love
without any intentions of loving them.

My intentions are pure.
I love your everything
and will share everything for sure.

# True Love

L – O – V – E

Such a simple word of only four letters
oh dear God what could be better.

L – O – V- E

Short in stature but tall in meaning
easily stated but hardly penetrated.
Love is caring and sharing boldly
without fear, unconditionally my dear.

L – O –V –E

Compromise and compassion should be worn like fashion
honest and trust is a must, not all this commercial lust.

L – O – V – E

Loving someone is a choice; your choice to hoist yourself to another
level where you can revel in the delight of what God intended no
pretending.

# War

I let it down against my better judgment, I let it down…
Dropped my defense, exposed now wearing this frown.

I knew better, I knew it was too much, too soon, too fast.

My heart took control, snatched a chance to declare its position
sitting there outside the fort uncovered, watch for the ammunition
loaded in heavy artillery, might have to abort this mission.

I knew better, I knew it was too much, too soon, too fast.

It seems at a glance all my dreams are shattered
my soul feels battered. War in love is no easy task.

Damnit! Where's my flask?

I knew better, I knew it was too much too soon, too fast.

# Addiction

My drug of choice is love
it keeps me flying high above.

Seeking the full essence of its power
consumes me, and just like that, I'm devoured.

Swept away on this roller coaster of life
losing to my own addiction,
while telling a story of non-fiction.

My drug of choice is love
and it fits like a glove.

My heart is wide open waiting for an intervention,
my heart requires so much attention.

My drug of choice is love
and I'm fully addicted.

Printed in the United States
By Bookmasters